D1710884

ABOUT THE AUTHOR

Hi! My name is William Barnard and I'm a 28 year old dad of three girls. Science and the solar system has always been interesting to me. So it only seems fitting that my first book be about that. My dog Charlie is my best friend and I love making stories of adventures he can go on. Follow along for our future adventures!

Charlie

EXPLORES THE SOLAR SYSTEM

This book is dedicated to Eliza, Grayce and Willow

Illustrated by:Shafiakanwal93

Table Of Contents

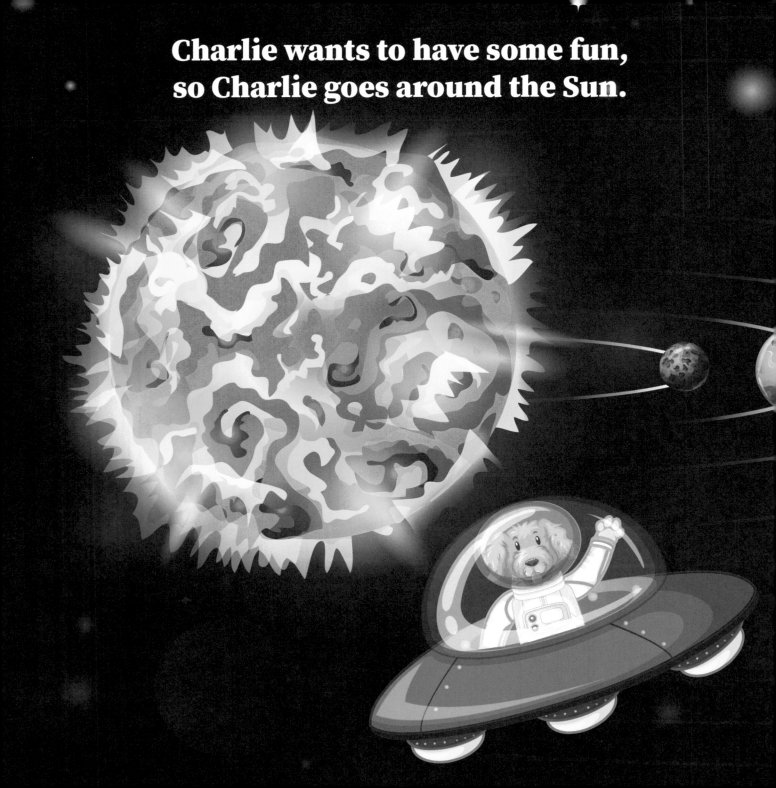

Charlie wants to have some fun,
so Charlie goes around the Sun.

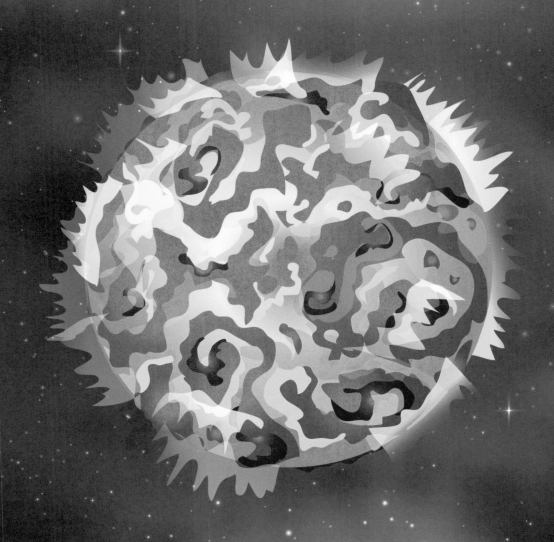

Did you know the Sun is over 4.5 billion years old? Without the Sun, there would be no Earth.

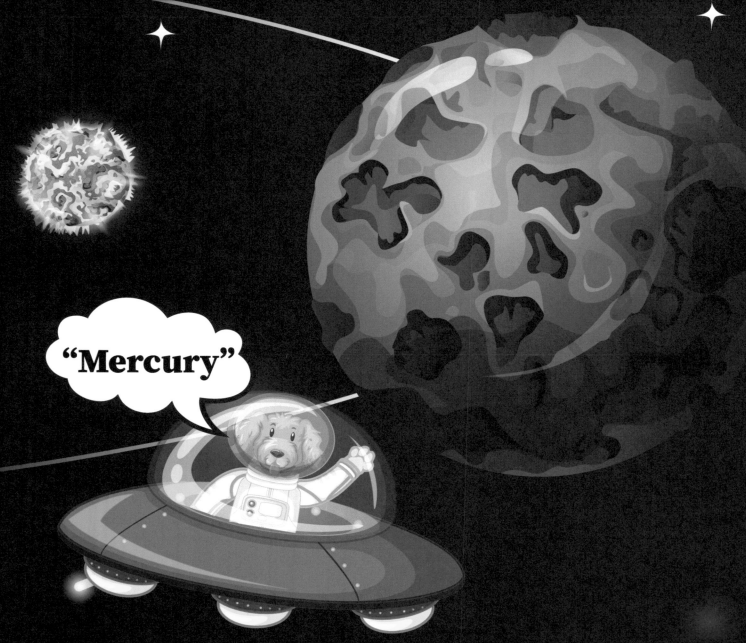

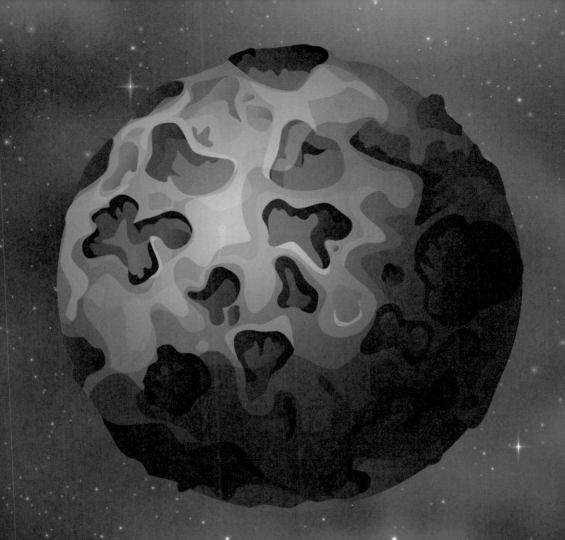

Did you know Mercury is also the smallest planet? It has the most craters out of any planet in our solar system.

Did you know Venus has year-long days, with only two sunrises in the year?

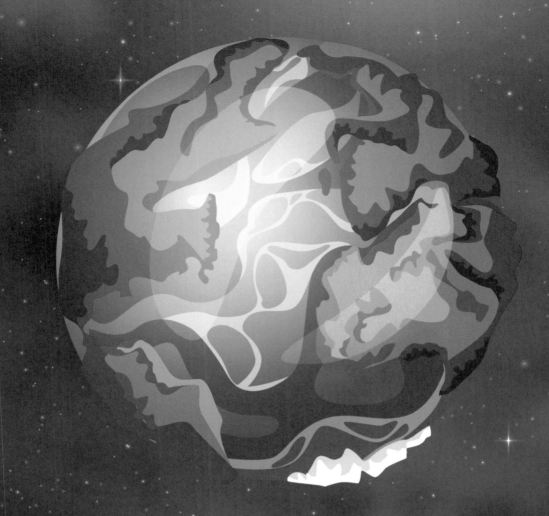

Did you know 71% of Earth's surface is covered in water, that contains over 400 species of sharks?

Did you know Mars can have huge dust storms? These can last for months and can also cover the entire planet!

Did you know Jupiter has rings? but they're too faint to see very well. Jupiter also has 80 moons.

Did you know you cannot stand on Saturn? It is not like Earth, because it is made mostly of gasses.

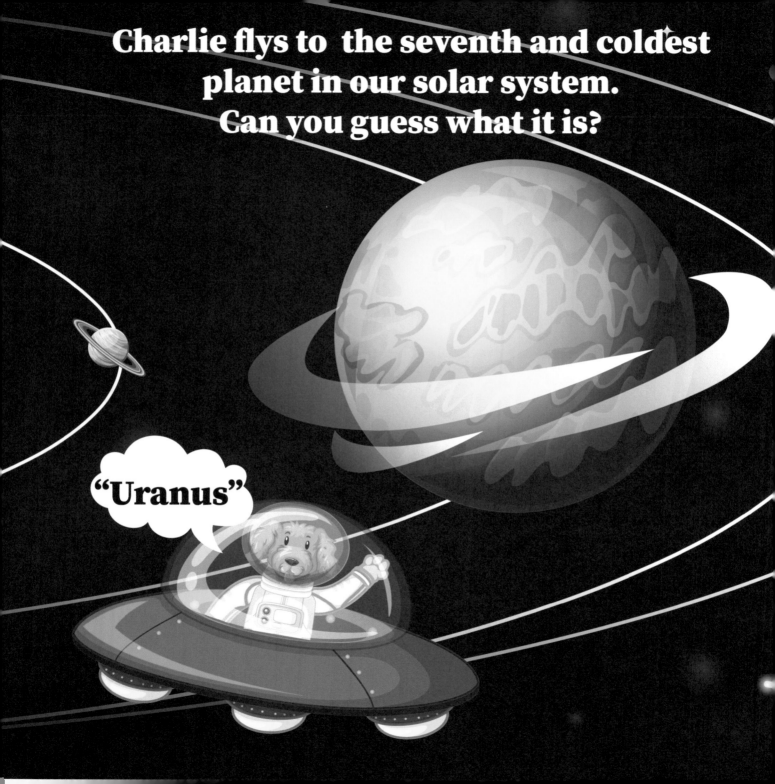

Did you know Uranus orbits the Sun on its side?

Charlie visits the icy giant the final planet in our solar system. Can you guess what it is?

Did you know Neptune has at least five main rings and four more ring arcs? These are likely clumps of dust and debris formed by the gravity of a nearby moon.

THE END

Made in the USA
Columbia, SC
16 December 2023